AF504387

Hi, my name is Chester, and I am two years old. I love to walk on sunny days, sniffing plants and flowers everywhere I go

{ 2 }

This place is getting crowded. There are lots of friends here who got lost or were abandoned by their families. It's sad, but I'm hopeful!

{ 3 }

That's why I hope I can adopt my next family soon. I want freedom! A bed of my own to sleep in, my own bowls for food and water.

{ 4 }

I like playing with people more than with toys. So far, none of the families who came to see me were the right fit

{ 5 }

I didn't like any of the families who came before, so I showed my teeth to let them know. My cute face doesn’t help when I try to show my disapproval!

{ 6 }

But today, I see a family waiting for me in the garden. Let me go closer and sniff. Ooh, I like how they smell!

{ 7 }

The lady looks a little scared of me. Let me rest my head on her lap. Ah, she's patting me! I can feel her love and care already.

{ 8 }

She's my new mom. I can feel it! Let me sniff the gentleman. He seems nice too. Yes, this is my family!

{ 9 }

I can’t stop jumping. I found my family! Hey friends, I’m going home!

{10}

Chester jumped into the car, ready for his new adventure. Suddenly, the car stopped. Where are we now?

{ 11 }

We're at a school! Oh my gosh, I got a big brother too! This day just keeps getting better!

{ 12 }

Life is awesome! Thank you, God, for helping me choose the perfect family!

About The Author

Lekshmi Kiran is a seasoned professional with a diverse career spanning project management, education, and media. With 16 years of experience in the project management field, Lekshmi has successfully led numerous initiatives, demonstrating her expertise in organization and leadership. For the past six years, she has shared her knowledge as a teacher in robotics and coding, inspiring young minds to embrace technology and innovation.

Lekshmi spent six years as a television anchor in India, where her passion for storytelling captivated audiences and honed her communication skills. This lifelong love for narratives has seamlessly woven into her current endeavors as an author, where she continues to craft engaging stories that resonate with readers.

Outside of her professional life, Lekshmi is a dedicated wife and mother to a son who is currently in college. She finds joy and companionship with her two dogs, Chester and Chico, who are cherished members of her family.

Balancing her multifaceted career with her personal life, Lekshmi remains committed to her passion for storytelling, always seeking new ways to connect with and inspire others through her work.

www.ingramcontent.com/pod-product-compliance
Lightning Source LLC
Chambersburg PA
CBHW041728100726
47973CB00010B/141

* 9 7 9 8 3 3 0 4 1 3 3 2 4 *